THE WILLIES

poems

Adam Falkner

Published by Button Poetry / Exploding Pinecone Press
Minneapolis, MN 55403 | http://www.buttonpoetry.com

—

Manufactured in the United States of America

Cover design: Kate Zaremba

ISBN - 978-1-943735-66-2

23 22 21 20 19   1 2 3 4 5

For my father

THE WILLIES

III.

"Mad lives is up for grabs."

—Ghostface Killah

* * *

"Change is not a threat to your life,
but an invitation to live."

—Adrienne Rich

I.

Willie Boy

Finally, the poem I will not write.
I am in fifth grade, wrestling
in a brush pile of dead leaves
with a now-dead friend. We paw
the hardening knots in each other's
gym shorts, laugh and writhe until
the leaf pile is no longer a pile
but a kicked-in hive of tiny heaving
lungs; soft stink of new sweat
and rotting wood. Six girlfriends
and a dissertation later, I wake up
in a tougher city with new friends
who remind me of my father.
I look at men with chiseled
jaws on loud trains in new ways,
or rather, old ways but with less
at stake. Wonder if they ever hover
their gaze over me for an instant
too long, too; if the flexed tricep
peeking from under my own black
t-shirt makes them dance their eyes
into pretend reading material, too.
I freeze snapshots of beautiful strangers,
pin them in the high-ceilinged hallways
inside me near the faces of everyone who
knows me by a different town and
a different version of my father,
none of which are of the Christmas
he got loaded and started yelling about
how gay people give him *the willies*,
rooted in "Willie-boy," or sissy—

a name I've tried fighting and drinking
and fucking away since sixth grade.
A badge I've tried burying amidst
the brass edges of ball fields
and rap songs. Still, from beneath
the goose down of this new bearded
man, soft snore into my shoulder's
right teacup, hairy thigh laid heavy
across my lap, I peck the first lines
of a poem I will not finish. Another
Willie. Sissy. It raises its hand, draws
a blank. Swells its chest, coughs soot.
Curls its fists. Slinks into the night.

Let's Get One Thing Halfway Straight: I have spent my entire life trying on costumes because no one told me I couldn't and the stakes were never that high which I've come to think is mostly what makes a white writer a white writer. The last time anyone referred to me by that name was exactly never but that's also the point. I am a queer poet. Child of an addict. Masquerading white boy. My best friend died and it was sad and these are the stories I water into bloom: camp counselor test cheat choirboy cypher rapper / scratch golfer honor roll pothead point guard / and Whitman says very well you contain multitudes but he was a white writer too. The not-so-funny thing about spending a life proving you aren't something is that any story that isn't *the* story is survival or more like a brick for laying until the wall is high enough that you're safe inside and you wake up and say whoops whose house is this who did I hurt to get here and is it too late to call for help.

Connor Everywhere But

after Jericho Brown

Connor on the 4 train, sports page rolled
          into a drumstick. Connor stretched out
shirtless on the front lawn, a football propped
          behind his head. Connor laughing against
the red brick of a café, head thrown to the sky
          like a sail snapped by the song of a quick
wind. Connor in The Daily News: *balcony*
          mishap, twenty-four flights, faulty railing.

Connor through the bottom of a pint glass.
          Connor through the crowd at West 4th,
fistful of fence in each hand. Connor in the
          glint of a windshield. Connor
hobbling on a kickstand crutch, swinging
          at stray frisbees, tree trunks. Connor
on Channel 7: *a good-hearted young man, filled*
          with hope, always whistling. Connor
drunk-leaning toward a woman at the bar,
          whispering a smile of green lights across
her face. Connor in black and white, frozen on a
          bookshelf. Tire-gravel high note of a blues
ballad, the scratch of stubble on another man.
          Connor collected cleanly into a shoebox.

Connor in the search bar. Connor on G-Chat:
          Invisible. Connor floating in the corner
of a cooler, tucked behind the last Newcastle.
          Connor circling in a breeze above the
Neversink, curling around the Hemlock; smoke in
          a dead room. Connor in a porcelain vase

on a mantle. Connor in poems that have nothing
          to do with Connor. Connor sitting shotgun
in the silent 4Runner on the way to his own
          funeral, bare feet propped on the dash.
Connor between eye-rubs on the couch before
          dawn, flashing in and out like an old-time
movie. Shower water running in the next room.

Intake

It wasn't as if my parents didn't understand.
The words *I'm dating a man* are not

easily confused.   I didn't say, *I'm spending
a lot of time with someone*, or *I'm going*

through sort of a phase.   But to their credit, I
also never said, *I'm gay*, either.   I thought

it might make them sad, encourage their
imaginations to sprint through all the dark

crevices of New York City with
its AIDS and artists.   Or worse, what

they could have done to make their son's first
quarter-century less quietly tortured

by locker rooms, less gluttonous with
chemicals and moments in back seats, storage

closets, leaf piles.   And how strange for their
eggshell love to not be enough.   To want

more volume.   More shattered glass.   More
phone calls from distant kin

whose holiday parties we're not welcome at
anymore.   How disappointing

to spend a decade collecting prop-up girlfriends
like lawn ornaments, scouring

for safety from this firework dud of a moment.
To deflate like a sad beach globe

when I finally work up the courage
to ask for violence, and all my mother can do

is smile.   Invite him home for the holiday.

My Father Is a Mansion

made entirely of myths,
each vaulted ceiling.
My father is a trophy
in a flock of empty frames,
fork in the most violent
of rivers. He is a detective.
Therapist. Sax player. A
nobody. Water walker. Weaver
whose mouth spills stories
like moths. Legend. He is
both arms flown
into the sky of a bomb
blast. Storm of a
thousand swallowed
keys. Candle in a cave
without an entrance,
his wine glass sloshes
into his lap
at red lights. Empty
groove in a mattress. Racket
of a hardback Dickens
through drywall. He helps
people fish inside themselves
for the right lie. He is
other women's names and
locked cabinets, one eye
cast over his shoulder for
shrapnel. He is vomit
on the bedroom carpet.
Scholar of the bomb blast
both arms around me.

He is made of myths and
keys and red lights and
other women. Pile of
snipped strings and snot
in a waiting room. Hardback
water walker. Fishing tale.
An elaborate entrance.

The Year the Wu-Tang Drops

Abbott Elementary has your parents on speed dial. Each time Ms. Baker calls to deliver the same tiresome news, you offer the same shrug. Interrogations at the kitchen table go in circles. They wonder why you would do such a thing, where you heard someone say such words. You say you are sorry, *It just—slips.* Each four-letter leaps into the air like a winged grenade: playground, art class. Spelling tests. Scared to tell them the secrets you've discovered lurking outside your older brother's bedroom, ear plated against his door like a stethoscope; how you thieve albums from his shelves like grapes in a grocery aisle to gorge in private; pound on repeat until each word is a mantra you can mumble in your sleep. Scared to say how "three continents away" this music feels pulsing through your small body, how fat your whiteboy eyes bulge at the sight of something unmistakably not

yours. How proud you are of
what Ghostface Killah is qui-
etly doing for your vocabulary.
Each weapon, a dangerous in-
sect you seal in its own glass jar.
How you roll it in your mouth, a
thick malt, tongue its chipped
edges, until certain of the exact
ways it can scythe a life in two.

A Tale of Two Cities

"Repression is the only lasting philosophy."
—Charles Dickens, *A Tale of Two Cities*

It did not seem strange to not fix the door:
it still opened, signaled my brother's want
for privacy when shut. It even seemed reasonable
he not mind the cannonball hole splintered in its
center—all the easier through which to call him
for supper, pass the phone or shoot
Nerf arrows when he was studying.
But what I remember most was the silence.
Like the alien in the movie whose humanness so
surprises the family they know not what to do
except dress it in old clothes, give it a plate at
dinner, have it play goalie at soccer practice.
Before long, the hole was part of the door itself,
scaffolding on a never-ending renovation. No one
ever gave it the title it deserved,
all 525 hardback pages of it, wedged
like a war spear for a week. No one said this is
what happens between men whose fathers are in
the water they drink. Football Saturdays and arm
chair rot. Who booze alone in the dark on back
porches. In the kitchen beneath the tick
of a broken ceiling fan. Bleachers at Little League.
Men hurt by the hands of other men. Who grieve
and love in the silence of shadows. No one ever
thought to yank the blade from the wound. Or
bothered to say its name aloud.

Thanksgiving

A loudspeaker announces departing
flights—I frown. The neon ticker at my
gate is a flashing infomercial for something
I already own and know to be a waste of money.
Nashville, St. Louis, Denver—all sound like
reasonable places to be today. My mother's
latest mantra: *No family is perfect.* She repeats
this quiet chant to remind herself she is not
losing some sort of game she is convinced
all American families play. I repeat it
to remind myself that she and I do not play
the same game. Today, for the first time,
Detroit is nothing more than a famous
sports town, a music mecca, the auto capital
of the world. We will sit and chew and
sleep. My father will talk about Michigan
football instead of AA, the Tigers in place
of rehab or any of the other women scattered
around his second and third lives
like pollen in the wind of a quick spring.
We will stare and remember and move. We
will say things like *Thank you* and *What a
clear morning* and *Is there a password
for the Wi-Fi?* All things I have said today
in an airport no closer to my home than *yes*
to *no, come* to *stay, Nashville* to the dinner
table I will give thanks for this afternoon—
the face at each delicate place setting,
its own walled country.

Flight 2331

Eight days since he fell
                24 stories, headfirst on the pavement
in the middle of 37th street. You are
                two martinis into a flight

300 miles above sea level, preparing to
                re-read a letter he sent you.
The last four digits of your credit card
                stuck to the plastic console above you

written in large, blue ink as if to warn:
                Keep an eye on this one. You knew there
would never be a right time
                for any of this. But here in 17C,

beside an ornery toddler, you wish
                you'd left his letter to burn a hole in your
jeans for one more day. The
                harder the child screams, the quieter

your head becomes. Gone is the rent check
                on your kitchen table, the laundry list
of unanswered emails, the collection
                of friends to whom you haven't broken

the news. Gone is even the slightest point
                of reference for why you are
on an airplane, where you are going, who cares
                about you. Were the plane's engine

to suddenly cough itself into Lake Michigan,
         you'd be more at peace with the world
than you are right now. You whisper this.
         Too loud. Think how non-triumphant

falling to one's death sounds anyway. The hand
         not nursing gin into your bloodstream,
a clenched weapon; it lightly pounds
         the armrest. Tears collect

in splashy globs on your tray table.
         You know this is just the tidewater.
This is just the beginning. You couldn't be
         any further from home.

My Grandma Calls Me Barack

Asks me by her bedside how
I'm enjoying the White House—
how that pretty Michelle
is doing, and if I've been able
to get any sleep. She says
she's ready to go home. *Just
unplug the spaghetti.* Smells
the meds in her milkshake
from a mile away. *No goodie
goo for me. No moxes for this
foxes. No trickson for this
Nixon.* I tell her the White
House is nice but it's a lot
of responsibility. I'm going
completely gray—as you've
probably seen. She clicks her
molars softly to match
the patter of the rain outside;
her eyes, a glazy gristle jumping
from TV to window to ceiling.
All those rooms, she sighs,
You must get lost. I tell her
I do. Almost daily. It's hard
to remember who I am
sometimes. *This health
care business. The whole gay
marriage thing?* These men
on magazine covers diving
into one another? Her eyes
stop skimming the room, settle
on the bottom of the 8th inning

in the corner. She calls me
Mark. Calls me Aaron. She
squints, points a bony finger
in my direction, skin slipping
from both sides like a wet
dishrag draped over an oven
handle. Calls me nothing.

Fishing the Little Pigeon

Once, when you were ten, you and he
wandered the bank of the Little Pigeon for hours
to find the perfect hole—a small cove buried

in a quiet elbow of the river: water black,
frighteningly cold. Fallen pines bridged
one side to the other, sunlight knifed through

trees. He was trying to teach you
the art of a good roll cast: start with
the rod tip down, let the current pull the line

to the darkest part of the river, then without
warning, snap the wrist like a whip upstream.
He stood behind you while you tried,

his large hands cupped around yours so
he could feel you feel the line plead
for trust—silence, the only rule. He wanted

to teach you the one art he knew
that *didn't demand a word*. To listen
to the trees with just your skin.

He motioned you upstream for a new fly
from his tackle, your grandfather's ornaments
of war. You peered inside the lid to find six cold

bottles, sweaty green glass impossibly
tempting, forbidden as a closed bedroom door.
Glancing over your shoulder, you opened one.

Poured it down your throat all at once
like a flame, as you'd seen on TV
a thousand times. You swallowed

the last wretched drop, rubbed the burn
from your lips. It would not leave.
You marveled at the kind of man it must take

to drink six in a single day, how such poison
didn't cripple him for the rest of his life,
the cardboard boxes in your garage

mountained with empty bottles must have taken
a lifetime of this burning to collect. How
he might be the strongest man in the world.

When he finally called your name—something
he'd not done in two years—you hid the glass
container beneath a clot of wet Tennessee mud,

stumbled to the water dizzy, teary.
Perched on the bank, his cast graceful as cello
music, he asked you for the fly he'd sent you after.

What took 30 long. Why you were crying.
He asked more questions in those 30 seconds
than you could answer with mere head nods

and shakes; afraid to curse the quiet
with the sound of your own voice, to be
the kind of boy it takes to break family

tradition—but you said nothing, protected that
legacy with a fury, nodding and shaking until your
neck ached. All the while another legacy, a darker

one, sliding into your life

                          without a word.

Intake

The counselor said he was unnervingly quiet
the night he was admitted.   He asked

why he was there, scoffed to the front desk about
doctors not needing doctors, slumped

into a sitting redeye slug on the waiting room
carpet.   Spent the next morning

wheezing up reasons to leave: water
the bushes, contact clients, speak

to his family, hold his wife.   After dinner,
during a meeting, he apologized to everyone

for being *so sick and rude and sad*.   Said he
finally understood why he was there,

why the work ahead could not happen
over night.   *Time to face the music.*

That midnight, staff found him on the shoulder
of the highway—same V neck

he arrived in, entire life stuffed into a ripped
Trader Joe's bag.   The whites of his eyes

flashing like bones in the dark.

The Year The Blueprint Drops

Once the street clears, you twist up a toothpick and adjust the volume on the stereo. Smoke. Seat reclined, you are a dope boy from Brooklyn, perusing the rat maze of your 'hood top down, wiretaps in your phones, feds staked behind your house—a life that couldn't be further from the cushy Midwestern one your parents gifted you: swimming lessons, choir practice, golf retreats, ice cream socials. The only explanation for how you are here—watching for cops *hopping out the backs of vans*, smoking your friend's expensive weed while he bobs in and out of a public housing development—is this: there is no manual on how to give privilege back, how to denounce a reach that stretches the ocean. No clean way to say: *I've had it. Take it all back. I wish none of this were ever mine.* "It" will always be yours, wherever you go. The ancient worlds you're trying to wrap your young, new-poison arms around are not black or brown or hip hop or poverty. They are merely not white. You know only what you do not want and you are dangerous beyond repair.

Kissing Your Shoulder Blade Is the Most Honest Thing I've Done This Week

I have read poems aloud
in barrooms about fresh heartache
       and addiction. Stood before
       a wide-eyed lecture hall, clapped

my paws and made it look
as earnest as a shoe shine. Sat
       at a glossy boardroom table
       in the clouds above 47th Street

with white people in power
suits and grinned like a scarecrow.
       Even told my therapist about
       the dark trunk I climb into

when I can't keep the shame
down, how it bubbles up
       past my fingers like mud
       around the sole

of a dress shoe—I'm a shitty gay, bad
boyfriend, ungrateful son.
       Morningside has woken
       me muzzled into the back of

your neck in a way I can't recall
the night shaping us. Sunlight
       blotches the hardwood,
       Dominican Spanish

wafts beneath the open window.
Your gentle breath grunts, tugs
          for light. Each freckled galaxy
          peppering your left shoulder

makes the shortest of my short
lists. I roam cluster to cluster:
          places to visit once I build up
          the chest hair to tell you

there is nowhere in this city
of gorgeous men I'd rather wake
          today, to the funk of a rough fuck
          the night before, ball of hot fur

at our feet—contemplating pounce
and ear lick, like he does, but gifting
          instead the silence to skate my lips
          along you, forgetting for the first time

in months how many holes
I have in this hungry, heartbroken
          body. And the lies I am always
          willing to tell to fill them.

L Train Rumor

Heard he was slap-boxing on the DeKalb
platform, lost his balance. The weight of his
backpack spun him drunk like a lopsided
hammock, the undertow tugging

at the heels of his Jordans. Heard he tumbled
back-first into empty Arizona cans, soggy
newspapers, urine. He was pushed by a student
at Bushwick High, no one saw the train.

Heard he was well-liked. Heard someone joke
he was chasing after a rat. He slipped trying to
slide around a homeless person. Heard that at first,
kids laughed. Facebook said he was gay.

He hadn't told his parents. He jumped.
Cinder blocks sniffed out his ankles like
bloodhounds. Heard he stood there, eyes shut,
people screamed. Heard no one knew him.

Heard by the time they pulled his body from under
the train, he was stiff as stale bread, muscled into
cardboard. Heard it took hours because the zipper
on his raincoat got stuck

beneath the wheels. Heard it didn't make the
Daily. Or the Post. Heard they closed the
Manhattan-bound L train for half the evening.
Heard people missed dinner with their families.

The Whitest Thing

Owning your own white guilt isn't cool
yet, so you stuff the soft parts of other kids'
cultures into your pockets until you believe it is
not there. You are a matching sweat
suit jukebox stocked with everything
from Ice Cube to OutKast, entire albums
memorized and coiled in the damp
of your mouth, gunfire into the air
above the school parking lot—and that
is as black as you think possible. Pulling blunts
the size of magic markers into your lungs
before school is black. Your dance routines
are black. They call you Justin Timberlake.
Sharpening your crossover is the blackest—
though you are the only whiteboy on the court
anyway. They call you Steve Kerr. Imagine
your whole body the color of a small freckle on
your right arm, how much more "you"
that really feels. And until someone tells you
otherwise, that is black, too.

It isn't that you don't know you are white.
Less white is all you really want to be—
you are sure there are good parts about having
white skin, too, even if you can't see them yet.
No one asks you where you came from,
how you got here—which is good because you
could not answer anyhow. You just appear.
With an insatiable hunger to touch things
that do not belong to you, a culture that fits
like a bed sheet. No one calls you carpet bagger,

tells you that you cannot place
your favorite things about black people
into a single bucket, try them on, parade
around on the front lawn for years
to feel better about a weight you cannot name,
until it is time to come inside for dinner.
So you do exactly that; dip your toe in
and out. Run when you must, stay when you
choose. And that is the whitest thing of all.

Men's Ten-Meter, London Olympics

Not all of them are gay, I say quietly.
Just to be real, that's not very likely.
This is the first of many summers in my
twenties where I defend the male body

to my family as a trial run. Sniff the air,
retreat. My father opens bottles
before the last is dry. *Of*
course they are. Just look at them.

My brother mumbles: I am *acting*
like a bitch. Teeth bare until someone barks.
Crystal is crunched into the carpet.
The meat is burned. My mother vanishes

for a walk. The television buzzes
a soft, glowing wash.
And no one watches the boy my age
make his lonely climb up the ladder. No one

sees him shake loose the nerves
from the ropy twine in his arms, ripple of muscle
waves up his back as he inches
onto the balls of his feet. Waits

for the right moment. Flashbulbs cocked.

II.

Straight

When I say he is a good-looking man,
I mean that objectively. As in anyone
who thinks otherwise might be so
homophobic that they themselves are
gay—and I am not gay, therefore,
I appreciate how others might be drawn
to certain features he holds. When
I say I find him handsome, again
I'd like to clarify: I think of him as
beautiful in that "girls love him" way.
How, if I were a girl, I might wait outside
his dressing room, too, write him letters,
too. However I am not, so I won't,
but I get it. And even this, said aloud
in this very room, a flag javelined deeper
into the cocksure certainty of my own
Budweiser. So straight, that is, that I could
say I think about his stubble against my neck
without your thinking this poem is about to
get gay as hell: that glorious scrape and push
of dueling jawlines, how I spend my
morning commute on the 2 train
wondering how our college soccer hips
might feel cutting into one another
in a corner, on the hood of a car in some
hipster neighborhood I do not live in.
Where no one knows me outside
this splintered park bench, these
rolled up jeans and tired black t-shirt.
This orange magic hour on the East River,

hairy tattooed arm laid lazy around my neck
like a hitching post. A giddy ribbon
unravels inside me each time
he cups my face in his palms.

Look At Me Now

Flash and footwork and gum chew.
Long hair and tardy and
postracial: even the humility
a sales pitch. *Honored*
to be here. Now watch me
wash in the fuss of this stage
light: miss girlfriends I do not
have. Ignore the one I do.
Hate a family whose love is
the reason I'm alive. Here are
lies that sound like water. Watch me
show up to the black tie in sweats
and Air Maxes, grin like
a pay day, beg, *clap while I flash*
the bones of another life. Fill
me with praise I can't sleep
without. Let me dare you
to ask if I work here between
slam scores and Sunday dinner.
Dance practice and football tailgates.
I work here: We are lower
class. Came up the hard way
with silver spoons and jazz
music. Nobody ever handed me
anything except boychoir and
National Parks and love caped
around me like a steel curtain. But
here are their drinking problems.
Their shattered marriages. The doors
they punch. The things they shout

across holiday parties. The humans
they wound. Here are their worst
mistakes, wandering around on all fours
in the sunlight. *Now look at me.*

His Name Was Eduardo and I only did him for Ariel and like three other people and only when they asked usually in our favorite last seat on the school bus. Eduardo was an enterprising young hairdresser from Miami with a heavy *lithp* and limp wrists and big hair which I'd always have one hand on maybe pulling it back or wrapping a towel around or tucking rollers into or misting with spray. I imagined him in skinny tracksuit polyester with jewelry like my grandmother's that rattled when you waved plus rings on his fingers that clinked against the cans when he used them— the point is I made people laugh. We had boyfriends all over South Beach who knew about each other and that got us in trouble but that was funny too because of sex and I was one of the last stops on the route so sometimes Eduardo and I got to strut down the bus aisle together and wave goodbye to all the empty seats.

Ronnie's Father Was the First Real Drunk I Knew

He'd apologize over and over as if it was
the only thing that would sober him. We'd laugh,
shrug it off as though just another Tuesday.
Sometimes he tried bribing us: *Stay*
a little longer, talk Michigan football,
listen to one of his stories about being
on the job and chasing a raccoon
out of someone's heating duct. He'd stuff
as many singles in our open palms as it took
to make him calm whatever hornet
takes home in a man's skull to make him drink
himself into a stupor on a weekday afternoon.
He only asked that we never tell
Ronnie's mother we had seen him *like this*:
sprawled out at the kitchen table
in his bath robe, mountain of Marlboros
smoldering in a pie tin. I can't remember
if it was because we were scared
of Ronnie's mom or because we knew something
no one else knew. But we never said a word.

Even when we started skipping school
for the few extra dollars he'd give us
to empty the cat litter, wash dishes,
clean the refrigerator. Even when we
let him sleep in the basement bathtub
on nights Ronnie's mom threw his things
into the street. Even when we watched
him flatten the mailbox in drunken rampage,
the wheels of his truck carving wet troughs
into the lawn. We peeked over our shoulders

for neighbors, propped the post back
into its hole and shifted conversation
toward girls in 5th period English. Or
when we spotted him five years later in line
at McArthur Shelter in one of Ronnie's
old Lions Starter jackets, cheeks wind-whipped,
clothes filthy and torn. We just kept our
eyes on the red light in front of us.
Noted only how clear the sky was,
how perfect an afternoon for a drive.

Intake

We head toward the far end of the field
to collect a lost kickball and simply

collapse.   Jigsaw cutouts laid
awkward atop one another, face up.

I don't know how or why we decide to fall here,
but I am surprised by his weight—like he might

crush me if we so much as giggle.   If we flutter
a muscle toward naming the weirdness

of it all.   To the rest of the playground,
only Jeff in bits, on his back

in a pile of rotting maples.   But I am
underneath panting for breath, learning

every inch of my body's thick
hum, my heart a whirring bike spoke.   My tiny

sex mashed into the ribs of his back.
From this moment, sixteen years will pass

before I'll feel the weight of a man
like this again.   It will be in the back seat

of a Jeep Grand Cherokee.   Pleather will stick
to the backs of our thighs and

I will not care that he does not know my name.
But here we rise and brush ourselves off, trek

across the field after the bell without a glance.
Tomorrow, I will flop here again for Jeff

to see.   Watch his hard gaze in any direction
but mine.   Take in the open air above.

Cool

The hardest part was always letting go.
Posted in my too-fly-to-dance,
what-if-she-laughs corner of puberty:
all Adam's apple and weed smoke,
stubble-free and jock mouth,
prepared for the melting of my cool
at the beat drop. It took courage
and patience for a DJ to garnish Michael
into an evening of high school booty music,
and since my seven-and-a-half-minute *Billie Jean*
routine was no good to a Dr. Dre beat,
I'd wait by the fringe of the floor
like a lion in tall grass for hours
until I finally got my turn. The hardest
part was remembering I had practiced
this before. In my living room.
Daily. Before my mother returned
from work, my rug-burned bare feet burrowed
into carpet. Turning with hairpin precision
to the baseline, capsizing holy and suddenly
plugged in. A waking puppet
all lock-step slide-glide
crotch-grab air-grind
pendulum knee-kick-perfect
and beautiful, like the first time
my friend made me snap my ankles
before a group of older boys
in the lunchroom. Reluctant, red-faced,
I threw down
every piece of dust cloud footwork I could muster

like gambling chips at a table I wasn't invited to,
breaking every heel-spin with toe-punch
and no apology. I moved like my cool
depended on it.

Sleeping Beside My Mother

We lie side by side in the bed my parents shared
for 37 years. Two thousand miles
from my own bed in Brooklyn, I am dwarfed
by the groove his heavy trunk has worn

into the mattress. Earlier today, we began
the task of readying for winter: hauled
in deck furniture, turned off the hose,
coiled it in the rafters. At the bank,

we met with a man who helped us shift
their assets. Changed the locks,
installed new alarms. The hardest war
to prepare for is the kind you fight without

admitting that it is happening. I watch
her chest climb and dip, match her breath to mine.
My body is a cavern slowly piling
with ghosts. I close my eyes and count.

If You Don't Know

after The Notorious B.I.G.

Shirtless and grass-stained, you scowl at
your own 12-year-old reflection in the
bedroom mirror. Strike your hardest L.L.
for the camera, grip the backs of your
own bird-blade shoulders like holds on a
climbing wall, taunt the child in the glass
to say something back. *Pictures on the
wall*, castle of crisp sneakers still in their
boxes, words that fit like strange origami
in your cavity-free mouth: the only white
kid you know who can do it like this.
And sure, people laugh. Call you fool.
After all, the public housing you boast of,
the *interviews by the pool*, minks you buy
your mother—all just a dream: gasoline
in an imaginary engine propelling you
away from the soft, pliable furniture of
your boring, suburban nest. But you
know very well who you are: tourist
walking circles in a city they did not
build. You study the shape your mouth
makes around *common* and *thief*, *dead*
and *broke*, until finally you reach the part
that is not yours to say—even whiteboys
like you who aren't *really* white but for
their ability to disappear, leap into the
wind, board a return flight when the
clock strikes homesick. You are the
source. The genesis of a new kind of
whiteboy: sticky paper for hands, fat with

guilt you do not have time to name, fitted cap like a parade mask. You roll the word around in your mouth like a jawbreaker. Slap it against the drywall of your bedroom, swallow its colonial flare like cheap whiskey. Add it to the growing pile of things you can never give back.

Intake

Outside on West End, November whips from
the river like a swarm of pebbles.   Passersby

tug coat collars around ears, penguin-shuffle down
blocks.   Six days ago, a hurricane

gulped the lowest lying neighborhoods, left some
of my students without homes, in

shelter lines, searching Facebook for family.
Still no power in the projects.   I tell

my therapist who isn't yet my therapist about my
dad's weird art room.   His recent

deck project.   The latest woman to go to the
press, patient to come forward.   All just

different shades of caulk to cake over the void of
an unexamined life.   I slouch like a slug

in a share-your-feelings arm chair.   Admit I do
not trust the cloak that therapists don but

also that I am here, picking through rubble,
champagne bathing in my own self-pity because

I do not know where else to go.   Still shopping
for the just-right lap to dump my boring gay

grief into.   Just need someone to hear me out.
I tell him he can be whoever he wants.

Definition of Privilege

Nathan and Davis had the wad of
bills we stole from Nathan's grand-
pa's work coat so when they led us
down the block to Hop-In we fol-
lowed because we were thirsty and
had no idea our friend Alex who
was black would minutes later
have his chest on the pavement,

> a stranger's hands scaling his
> waistline and thighs while the rest
> of us would watch from the
> sidewalk with our tongues
> pretzeled like the barrels of
> cartoon rifles and I was nine years
> old on the verge of a fifteen-year
> obsession to prove I was not
> whatever it was that kept me off

> the pavement alongside Alex, first
> by quitting classical piano lessons
> and growing my hair out and
> studying the blues then traveling
> across continents with groups of
> quasi-guilty Christians to build
> schools in Peru or community
> centers in Israel or soccer fields in

Mexico or Whereverthefuck and
then working up the nerve to rock
matching track suits every day in
the upper lot at Pioneer High
School and basketball jerseys two
sizes too big and start drinking
forties of Old English malt liquor
like Ice Cube with kids who lived
in Eagle Park and West Maple and

reciting Too Short verses to my
crush at the bus stop where I
started smoking so much weed
before school that I got suspended
for vomiting in the trash can dur-
ing my third period English class
and had to go to summer school

which I really used as an
opportunity to distribute the first
of many mixtapes in my very seri-
ous rap career that I swore would
be my "ticket outta here" on which
I used spoonfuls of words my
mother didn't understand until I
landed in college and registered for
classes where I was the only white

person and a professor asked me to share the earliest memory I had of race so I told the story of Nathan and Davis and the stranger's hands and she asked why whiteness made me so uncomfortable and I said, *It doesn't* but then I said, *Because I don't ever think about it* and

she replied, *Not having to think about something sounds like an amazing privilege* and then I started seeing kids who looked just like me (everywhere) whose lives were bending into knots like the barrels of cartoon rifles just to prove they weren't whatever it was

that kept me off the pavement when I was nine years old which is to say guilty for something they didn't do which is to say *I never owned slaves I'd never say the N-word I don't see color anyway* or I don't really have a race which is to say the option of silence.

It's Tricky So Stay With Me: I crushed on the girls who dated the boys I crushed on which I understand seems inefficient but really it did the job. I loved Jeff or at least from my desk behind him in third period I liked imagining my palm slapped around the buzzed cowlick on his neck and Jeff asked Tasha to a dance which I knew to mean that Tasha and I should hook up it's not that complicated if you think about it. I loved Evan or at least the way pool water clung to his trunks and his thigh hairs when he climbed out of the chlorine and he got head from Michelle Cantor that summer behind the equipment shed so I gave her my virginity we thrashed around in the dead darkness of a linen closet our bones clacked against the wood floor until there wasn't much else to say.

you are an exception to the rule. Other kids just don't seem to understand how delicate the dance, how to fold their skin like a cape into a square the size of a coloring book, tuck it in a letter drawer for a rainy day—for when being black finally goes out of style. They float through the hallways of your overcrowded high school like silly birthday balloons; sweat suits three sizes too-big, basketball jerseys drape their skinny frames like lamp shades. You can't even look them in the eye when you pass—your glance scampers for the nearest exit to avoid even the slightest exchange because you, with your a cappella smile and your black girlfriends and knowledge of civil rights history, are different. You know every word to the classics and the details of their liner notes, too. Your dance moves are cleaner than you'd ever show your mother. You know more about the African Diaspora than most of your black friends—and these other clowns haven't the slightest clue what they're up against. They don't know how silly they look. They don't know appropriation is a contest they have to win to be exempt from. They don't know you've already won.

Intake

Naked and drunk at a construction site
in Brooklyn could not have been
what my therapist meant

when he said I'd figure it out
someday.   How if I just loosened
my grip and stopped trying to control

things, I might even surprise myself.   So I
stripped down, too.   Said yes
to second-date Oliver, the tequila-whipped

blubber that became of our legs, bicycles
locked and abandoned against street planters.
Yes to the chain link he pulled back

and the perch of concrete jutting into the East
River.   We scratched the jeans
from each other's salt-caked bodies,

center court spectacle in an arena of luxury
condos on the rise.   But it was I who first
said yes to the filth, oil slick and cake-batter

churn.   Promise of a lurking unknown.
Baptism by soot clot.   I briefly weighed
my own death: a washing of 25 years

ending in an obituary clipping.   Rip current
and toxins in the blood.   Worthless hospital
bill for my mother to deal with.   Or just a

hangover.   Just a gouged-open foot
in need of stitches in the morning; new language to
learn.   Another shot at a bright new life.

III.

Adoption

There are men whose mouths
      my tongue has lapped through.

Whose stink and hum I've tasted
      in barrooms too slicked over

with whiskey and Whitney
      for anyone to be the wiser.

Who I could not help but offer
      outstretched in my slight hands

when mother asked, now that
      Whatshisname and I are done,

What's next? Meaning: is dick
      the thing you're settling into

and onto and if so, *That's fine,*
      but are you thinking of adoption?

Tonight I think of the streetlight
      on South Portland, how it stripes

a barber pole onto his dancer's
      back. Whose hands around neck

mid-thrash, tongue wormed deep
      into the well of me, whose prickly

chin I gulp, gnaw—roar of laughter
      into morning. I think of that feral

crave in a man's eyes. How it clings
          and does not give when it wants

what I want. Says this, the only open
          door. Walk. Wave

to our families, say, *Thank you*—
          or not—and spring into the wind

of another stiff body, say, *Teach
          me to land*. Take me into your fold.

Flock. Mouth. Humid crash and cave
          of skin. Spin me a new name.

Shove me into the sun.

Intake

SeaWorld is a busy place, so it sort of makes
sense.   Park security is nice.   They feed us
apples and popcorn while they search high and
low, megaphones and flashing golf carts.
They help us write postcards to
our parents.   *Dear Mom, Grandma is here*
somewhere we just don't know where
yet.   Also we got hats!   They find her
dancing in the empty sundrenched bleachers at
Dolphin Cove, yelling for Shamu.   At the
health center, they say heat stroke.
Dehydration and empty stomach.   They let
us coat our bellies with turquoise candy corn
while the grown ups talk on the other side of the
glass.   They give us fluffy manatees that we
slap each other with instead of cuddle because we
aren't six.   Aren't so young that we
do not know when the party is over—or even that
ours is the blood it rages through.

Joey From Dawson's Creek Was My Beard which if you don't know means she was my prom date my monster truck my main squeeze rumor swatter. All I had to do was leave my locker ajar for her scotch-taped image to yell to all of B Hall that there was nothing to see here after all just Joey at the end of a dock. Joey in a field of daisies. Joey in Bobbi makeup ads and stepping onto a red carpet. Obviously the gayest thing ever but let me get to the point: Joey wasn't real except that she taught me how simple it was to hide in a look and a laugh or to hold hands at the back of the bus and kiss in the smoky basements of parties and on the hoods of cars in stadium parking lots or for how to say faggot and how to avoid the boys whose air I could feel come off them and toward me when they walked. Another way of saying this is god I'm just so sorry. There were just so many. And I didn't even watch the show.

As Long As You're Out

Honestly, I'd prefer white wine. If they have it.
Plus an antique cigarette holder with "Aubrey"
etched in the side. This room here is for my
elephant, but I'm not sure it's big enough—
marble imported. As long as you're out,
could you bring back a satchel of lambskin
or something? I have a lot of "feelings"
I'd like to stuff in an expensive place.
I'm good for it. Just put me in a chair
and raise me the fuck up. Make sure
we're recording because this year could be a
moon landing. World war. Jurassic Park.
Might spend it in a Raptors jersey or my house
tights. Not sure yet—just *all out* is what I'm
thinking. Bring me a bucket of Molson Ultras.
Tuna sandwich the way my mom makes it, lightly
toasted. Squad of carrier owls to get the word out.
Bring me two days' stubble on a man
with wild eyes. Crack the truffle butter and coat
my chest with it—if you *need* to ask, go ahead but
as long as you're out, could we touch
up the treble on the parts where I'm crying?
Where I'm soft and weepy about that ex
I lose sleep over? Are we rolling here? Let's
pay a stunt pilot to throw my name in the clouds.
This the shit I wanna come out to. Film me while I
jump into the gust of all this gold.

Holden's Poem

after Frank Ocean

Let me first say that I wrote this entire poem
in my head while faking small talk

with a man whose company I did not enjoy.
Stared right through his pretty face

at the exposed brick behind him, smiled
and nodded like a dumb dog. I want to be honest

with you early so you'll believe me
when I tell harder truths toward the end. The food

was fine, but we were there because our feathers
needed ruffling, ghosts needed raising; he

said something about E-40 and we
were in a library searching for reasons to let

our parachutes loose. We were there to tilt
the room with wine until we missed our exes

enough to wear a groove into the cherry rug
on my living room floor. I would say

this poem is not about sex, but I already look bad
so I might as well admit that I've been wandering

these days. In and out of doorways
and offices and strange living rooms, new haircuts

and new people, corny Irish pubs
and libraries gluttonous with *super rich*

kids with nothing but loose ends whose leather
I envy from across the quad until I find myself

seated neatly at a dinner table with one
of them, and it isn't long from there

that I slowly start being myself again and thinking
about other people and exit signs and rivers and

anything I can float on and grass that grows
just high enough for me to stand completely still

and swirl into white noise like a drink order
in a noisy bar. It isn't long from there that I

wonder what's next. Who else is coming to this
barn dance. How long do we have to wait.

The Abandoned

The box fan chugs like an old lung;
you thumb through the graveyard of
poems you could not save. All share the air
of a day not unlike this one, when everything
you peck washes up on the same grief-fattened
shore. How even moments as "yours" as
the sound of chain-link nets at Burns Park
are intruded upon: he is leaning from a car
window, barking a bouquet of colorful
curse words; lying beside a campfire
with a bottle of Irish firewater wedged
between his thighs; baying at his pinstripe
royalty on a flat screen. Or he appears
mid-fall, morning coffee suspended in the air
as the balcony crumbles beneath him,
railing just out of reach. *Connor can't show up
in every poem*, you've thought. You don't
want to be one of those *sad poets*. But today
you are overcome by the evidence—
each time you've tried to swat him
out of your work, shoo his persistent heart
from flashing into your stanzas like a gust
of good wind. Poems scatter the floor
like junk mail, abandoned at the mere waft of
your friend all because you don't want
to be a *sad poet*. The dog nuzzles
into your elbow as you weep and start
in on your new job as a sad, sad poet—
who knows there is no handbook for
how to house a downpour. Its incessant
knocking. Every door flung open at its hinge.

Preparing the House

Sean tells me his father is dead,
and the story of how he left
one glorious drink at a time. He
spiraled out of this earth behind
the wheel of a Ford pickup and enough
cavalry clattering through his blood
to overtake a small nation. I
tell him how most days I wait
for the phone to ring with news
of the same thing happening
to mine. And then we lay
without a word beneath the
covers, still learning the shape
of each other's bodies, what
fits where—all in an antique
bed built for a child half our size.
After a moment he reminds me
that at least I can prepare for it—
the spiraling. A soft dog
snarl surfaces in my stomach,
unaware that we were competing
with our dead or soon-to-be-dead
drunk dad stories, but he has a
point, and I am defensive. I tell him
so. These days, my dad and I
don't talk about the elephants—
their always-there presence,
grazing in and out of each room.
Instead we lob each other bread
crumbs like sports scores and
headlines and see what sticks.

And it is work to think of this
small talk as anything other than
futile, like chopping at the rind
of a redwood with a bread knife,
while my mother lumps over
a friend's kitchen table with her
head in her hands and steely,
tree-ringed table coasters drooping
beneath her eyes. But the crumbs are
what Sean reminds me he'd do anything
to share with his own father now.
We are wrapped in one another's
warm spots, his breath a calming tide
against my neck. I don't know
him well enough yet to know if this
is something he does—the lifting up
of the hood and letting men peer
down into his scarred and tarry motor.
I will learn that it is not, and it will be
this fact that begins to pull my body
closer into his like a cargo ship
trudging into the halo of a lighthouse
beam. Just as I will also learn,
once the scotch has been
kicked, our clothes strewn about
the living room, the fire dwindled
to a soft brood, once the stones have
been rolled away from the mouths
of both our caves and only I want to
walk deeper down, what it feels like
to talk about the Knicks' losing record
instead of asking him to travel the world
with me. To *thunk* backgammon pieces

and hike through the pines in silence
at dusk instead of telling him that I
might be falling in love. But here,
months before I'll know the art of
grieving a man before he is gone,
of stealing and storing bits of him
in glass jars before the clouds come,
he tells me to call my father in the
morning. *Ask him about whatever*
and listen. Before long, I won't know
which man I mourn most, just that
the basement is beginning
to stack to the ceiling with boxes
from both their lives. Or all their
lives. That this shadowed room and
beard sweat and chorus of raccoons
chirping outside is a box
of its own. And that tomorrow
we'll begin boarding up the windows
with small talk. One tiny nail at a time.

Gospel

after Philip Levine

The gentle hum and flicker of a dingy gym light,
thin film of dirt from the school day dusts the
hardwood like beach sand, bleachers littered with
candy wrappers and homework. I sit with my back
flat against a faded blue mural by
the class of '86. The tenth period bell sounded
hours ago. The building completely still
but for the blind head of a janitor's broom
echoing four hallways away. I don't ask myself
what I'm looking for. I did not come for answers.
I came to feel the stick of leather against my
palms, leave the world I live in for an hour, grant
my body permission to forget and remember itself.

Tucked in my gym bag at center court
is an article by a person I've never met. It
bears news of my father that I can do nothing to
stop. I lace up my sneakers like they are maps
to the only place where people know my name.
Douse their rubber soles in my own dry spit
until they're squeaky and young—then it begins:
I cut and curl and fan out hard against a sea
of imaginary defenders until the floor is covered
in tiny droplets, until I've snapped the net clean
over a hundred times, sharpened my crossover
back into an axe head, head fake into a ghost and
the violent wind of the world is circling laps
at my feet. For the moment, nothing but this will

do. I am suspended like a song in a mason jar.
Weightless as an outlaw.

for Ed

Intake

My father started painting to even out the meds.
On long days when their syrupy undertow
beckoned him into the center of the earth,
he took to my childhood bedroom
to set the walls ablaze with cityscapes.   In
place of the rap posters and playbills were
canvases caked over in muddled browns and
blues.   Half-squeezed tubes of neon
strewn about desks, spools of spiny wire
gobbed with dried paint, each tiny window
clumped shut in blood orange.   Buildings
bullying into clouds of pond-algae.   Bizarre
bridges to nowhere, crisscrossed rivers,
moats stacked like oddly shaped bowls.

At first, I was frightened.   Froze in the door
frame with movie flashbacks of
mania on the loose: newspaper clippings
of obsessed-over crimes decorating the walls, cat
food in the corner.   But how dishonest it would
be to remember this as such.   For years, I've
sleuthed those portraits for a story that lines up:
cities he never had the strength to move to, bridges
he lacked the courage to leap from—anything
but a man trying to stay alive for
his family.   For that story never quite fit.
Because what then of all the poems?   The
paintings?   This skyline I
claim as sanctuary?   Harbor I ached toward,
both sails full?

Poem for the Lovers at Pickerel Lake

They plunge into one another's starving mouths
as though drawing venom from a snakebite—
sog beneath the surface like flooded sponges,
strands of blonde swaying like stray kelp.
From my lawn chair, I squint at the mockery
they make of gravity, how little they must know

                of its dodgy, dumb logic; ruthless
                stray lightning. This week I've watched it
                tease a 16-year-old into burying her body
                in couch cushions and fry grease; whisper
                one friend onto the guard rail of a bridge; sail
                another through 24 stories of darkness

onto a piss-soaked sidewalk. And still
there is nothing I can yell across this mirror
to warn them of what waits, should they breathe
too deep, laugh too hard, kiss too long, slurp
too full of one another. Nostalgic for the armor
of youth—so rind-thick, it is not even there—

                I mumble them courage in their discovery:
                nothing stays weightless forever. They bob,
                latch a tight vacuum at the lips, spilling with
                answers and no safer place to keep them. Lower
                and lower, they slip into the rippling. Until finally,
                without a sound, they are free.

Get Well Soon from Riverside Church

It has been 15 years since I last walked
into a church and meant it, sat beneath the gaze of
stone saints and prayed for anything
other than a new pair of basketball sneakers.

But I am here on my father's birthday, huddled
in the last pew with one leg toward the door
like someone might catch me, rattle an icy finger
in my direction and remember my name from

another life. I, the traitor. I, the walkaway.
But where else to take all these questions
of fathers and sons and ghosts that have haunted
the holy out of both of you—he, eight states away

speeding to and from his own trial
with a wine glass nuzzled in his lap
and a family shrinking in the rearview,
and I, here, on a cold day in December, driftwood

in this sacred stale cave, wishing I were still in the
bed of the man I woke with and courageous
enough to tell my father his name. And this, the
Great American Dad Story. This Everyone Aches

To Be Their Father Until We Grow Up
And Become Them story. Until it is we who are
hunched over toilet seats, vomit draped
from the mouth like a silk scarf; or we

who keep silent about the stories we know
will save our ticking lives, bury secrets like animal
bones until they gulp us whole; we who build and
set ablaze our own homes, string together lies

like bed sheets from which to rappel. But lest this
unravel into yet another poem wherein
the author pleads genetics, pleads, *Damnit if it
weren't for this booze and silence.* Because after

all, I am here, stealing a moment to hold him up.
Scared to admit that I might still believe
in miracles—raising of the dead, the turning of
water into, well, you get it—that I need to believe

he can jump back in the saddle. Stay
with us awhile. So happy birthday, dad. Please get
well. Please keep moving. His name is Sean. He'd
love to meet you. I talk about you all the time.

NOTES

The opening epigraph by Ghostface Killah is from the song "Can It All Be So Simple" from The Wu-Tang Clan's *Enter the Wu-Tang (36 Chambers)*.

The opening epigraph by Adrienne Rich is excerpted from an essay included in *On Lies, Secrets and Silence: Selected Prose*.

"One Thing Halfway Straight" references Walt Whitman's poem "Song of Myself."

"Connor Everywhere But" is after Jericho Brown. It draws inspiration and structure from the poem "Derrick Anything But."

"The Year the Wu-Tang Drops" is in reference to the Wu-Tang Clan's *Enter the Wu-Tang (36 Chambers)*.

"A Tale of Two Cities" references and borrows language from Charles Dickens' *A Tale of Two Cities*.

"The Year the Blueprint Drops" references Jay-Z's *The Blueprint* and borrows language from the song "U Don't Know."

"Look At Me Now" borrows its title from Chris Brown's song by the same name.

"If You Don't Know" references The Notorious B.I.G.'s *Ready to Die* and borrows language from the song "Juicy."

"By the Time The Chronic Drops Again" is in reference to Dr. Dre's *The Chronic 2001*.

"Adoption" draws inspiration from Aaron Smith's poem, "After All These Years You Know They Are Wrong about the Sadness of Men Who Love Men." The phrase "whiskey and Whitney" references Whitney Houston and has been borrowed as the title of a drag karaoke event in New York City.

"As Long As You're Out" references Drake's *Nothing Was the Same* and borrows language from the song "Furthest Thing."

"Gospel" is after Philip Levine. It borrows its title from Levine's poem by the same name.

"Holden's Poem" is after Frank Ocean. It draws inspiration from *Channel Orange* and borrows language from the song "Super Rich Kids." It also draws inspiration from J.D. Salinger's *Catcher in the Rye*—the title of the piece is in reference to Holden Caulfield.

ACKNOWLEDGEMENTS

Grateful acknowledgement to the editors of the following publications in which some of the poems in this collection first appeared, sometimes in earlier forms and under different titles:

Amazon's Day One Literary Journal: "Intake"
Anti—: "My Father Is a Mansion"
Assaracus: "The Waiting Rock," "Straight," "My Grandma Calls Me Barack," "Preparing the House," and "Adoption"
Corium Magazine: "Flight 2331"
Diode Poetry Journal: "Intake" and "Men's Ten-Meter, London Olympics"
FRiGG Magazine: "Poem for the Lovers at Pickerel Lake"
Painted Bride Quarterly: "Connor Everywhere But"
Resisting Arrest: Poems that Stretch the Sky: "The Definition of Privilege"
The BreakBeat Poets: New American Poetry in the Age of Hip-Hop: "If You Don't Know"
The Other Journal: "Cool"
Thrush Poetry Journal: "The Year the Wu-Tang Drops"
Uncommon Core: Contemporary Poems for Learning and Living: "The Whitest Thing," "Ronnie's Father Was the First Real Drunk I Knew"
Union Station Magazine: "No Sleep Till"
Vinyl: "Intake" and "Look At Me Now"
Winter Tangerine: "Willie Boy" and "Holden's Poem"
Word Riot: "Intake" and "Men's Ten-Meter, London Olympics"

Some of these poems appeared in the chapbooks *Adoption* (Diode Editions, winner of the 2017 Diode Editions Chapbook Award) and *Ten for Faheem* (Penmanship Books, 2014).

"The Definition of Privilege" was originally published in coursework curricula for graduate programs at the University of Washington, Columbia University's Teachers College, and the State University of New York, Oswego.

An early iteration of "The Whitest Thing" appeared in performance on an episode of *The Steve Harvey Show* for the National Broadcasting Corporation (NBC).

GRATITUDE

This book owes its arrival to a great many people. In some ways, I am a different person than the one who wrote some of the earliest poems in this collection, and am fortunate to have been loved and held up by a family and chosen family of artists and educators and activists and wanderlusters and queers and queens who fit and do not fit, are seen and still unseen, who understand the value of what it means to find a way through and leave the door open behind them—all of whom have pushed me to be a more courageous actor in my own life. Neither this work nor I would be possible without these folks, and countless others—and goddamn am I ever lucky. Brief but wild gratitude:

To the constellation of writing friends and editors who studied and pushed this book in its many forms: Jeanann Verlee (my forever editor), Jon Sands, Hanif Abdurraqib, Shira Erlichman, and Paul Tran. And to Mahogany L. Browne (my forever captain), Carlos Andrés Gómez, Angel Nafis, and Lauren Whitehead. This book does not exist without your companionship.

To north stars Patricia Smith, Saeed Jones, Dr. Cornel West, Aracelis Girmay, sam sax, Andrew Solomon, Bill Ayers, Bob Hicok, Patty Paine, and Bryan Borland for their words of support and wisdom along the way.

To further mentors and friends and heroes and collaborators whose tenderness, brilliance, and foolery I have been sustained by: Yolanda Sealey-Ruiz, Caroline Rothstein, Lynne Procope, Sofia Snow, Jive Poetic, Rico Frederick, Roya Marsh, Reed Swier, Eboni Hogan, Geoff Kagan Trenchard, Phil Kaye,

Carvens Lissaint, Michael Cirelli, Emily Kagan Trenchard, Michael George, Francisco Tirado, Paul Frederick, Will Hogan, Idrissa Simmonds, Sarah Kay, Alex Cuff, Shannon Matesky, Arhm Choi, Samantha Thornhill, Elana Bell, Gabriel Ramirez, Eve L. Ewing, Clint Smith, Aaron Samuels, José Olivarez, Nate Marshall, Molly Raynor, Mariama Lockington, Franny Choi, Karl Iglesias, Camoghne Felix, Aziza Barnes, Joshua Bennett, Maggie Ambrosino, Olivia Worden, Whitney Bates-Gomez, Jayson Smith, Philip B. Williams, Crystal Valentine, Christian Howard, Shanelle Gabriel, Marissa Lewis, Morgan Parker, Danez Smith, Cristin O'Keefe Aptowitcz, Patrick Rosal, Willie Perdomo, Bob Holman, Marc Bamuthi Joseph, Rafael Casal, Daveed Diggs, Chris Walker, Nathalie Costa Thill, Kathy Engle, JoAnn Hunter, Dick Scanlan. To my kind and encouraging dissertation advisors Ernest Morrell, Christopher Emdin, Laura Smith and Robert Fullilove. And more beloveds: Steve Strauss, Desmond Wilson, Micah Bartelme, Johnny Floyd, Lexi Cariello and the Cariello family, Elisabeth Mason, Phyllis Blumenfeld and Toby Citrin, Gale Spak, Julia Matsudaira, James Stair, Connor Donohue and the Donohue family, and more and more and more.

To the organizations and communities that granted unique space for me and this work to emerge: SupaDupaFresh and Ode to Babel, The Dialogue Arts Project, Urban Word NYC, The Pahara NextGen Fellowship, The Public Theater and the #BARS Workshop community, the ever-expanding Communion family, The Adirondack Center for Writing and the Anne La Bastille Residency Program, Commonplace Podcast, Queer Cinema Club, The Poetry Gods Podcast, Arts InsideOut, Corner House, The Nuyorican Poets Café, The Neutral Zone, Columbia University's Teachers College, Vassar College, The

University of Michigan's Program on Intergroup Relations, Diode Editions, Button Poetry.

To my first actual factual teacher, Jeff Kass—and to the many that have followed.

To the countless students I've had the privilege of working alongside at the Grand Street Campus, the Academy for Young Writers, Urban Word NYC, Vassar College, Columbia University's Teachers College, and elsewhere. Many of these poems were developed in dialogue with these young people.

To Sam Cook, Hitomi Wong, Nikki Clark, and the entire team at Button Poetry for believing in and fighting for this book. To Kate Zaremba for her brilliant cover art and generous design support.

To Charlie for your patience. Your good heart. The many ways you continue to help me see. The model that is your unshakable hustle.

To my family for receiving the stories I tell about us with grace and compassion. My father, who continues to show up and fight. My mother who makes every room better because she is in it. Nate for always showing the way.

And thank you, dear reader, to you. This is hardly a book without you. And now it is yours.

ABOUT THE AUTHOR

Dr. Adam Falkner is a writer, educator, and arts & culture strategist. He is the author of *Adoption* (winner of the 2017 Diode Editions Chapbook Award) and his work has appeared in a range of print and media spaces, including Painted Bride Quarterly, Anti—, Thrush Poetry Journal, on programming for HBO, NBC, NPR, in the New York Times, and elsewhere. A former high school English teacher in New York City's public schools, Adam is the founder and executive director of the pioneering diversity consulting initiative the Dialogue Arts Project, and special projects director for Urban Word NYC, in which capacity he oversees the New York City Youth Poet Laureate program and the organization's partnerships with corporate and cultural institutions across the country. Adam has toured the United States as a guest artist, lecturer and trainer for thousands of students, educators, and culture workers, and was the featured performer at President Obama's Grassroots Ball at the 2009 presidential inauguration. He holds a Ph.D. in English and Education from Columbia University.

OTHER BOOKS BY BUTTON POETRY

If you enjoyed this book, please consider checking out some of our others, below. Readers like you allow us to keep broadcasting and publishing. Thank you!

Neil Hilborn, *Our Numbered Days*
Hanif Abdurraqib, *The Crown Ain't Worth Much*
Olivia Gatwood, *New American Best Friend*
Donte Collins, *Autopsy*
Melissa Lozada-Oliva, *peluda*
Sabrina Benaim, *Depression & Other Magic Tricks*
William Evans, *Still Can't Do My Daughter's Hair*
Rudy Francisco, *Helium*
Guante, *A Love Song, A Death Rattle, A Battle Cry*
Rachel Wiley, *Nothing Is Okay*
Neil Hilborn, *The Future*
Phil Kaye, *Date & Time*
Andrea Gibson, *Lord of the Butterflies*
Blythe Baird, *If My Body Could Speak*
Desireé Dallagiacomo, *SINK*
Dave Harris, *Patricide*
Michael Lee, *The Only Worlds We Know*
Raych Jackson, *Even the Saints Audition*
Brenna Twohy, *Swallowtail*
Porsha Olayiwola, *i shimmer sometimes, too*
Jared Singer, *Forgive Yourself These Tiny Acts of Self-Destruction*

Available at buttonpoetry.com/shop and more!